# Table of Contents

## Look For These Other Books in This Series

*101 Essays to Empower You to Rise & Thrive*
*101 Essays to Empower You to Up Your Game*
*101 Essays to Empower You to Build Momentum*
*101 Essays to Empower You to Limitless Reach*
*101 Essays to Empower You to Peak Performance*
*101 Essays to Empower You to The Winning Edge*
*101 Essays to Empower You to Live Unstoppable*
*101 Essays to Empower You to Achieve Greatness*
*101 Essays to Empower You to Break Barriers*

# Introduction

This book comes from the insight and creativity of Frank Agin.

Who is Frank? He is the founder and president of AmSpirit Business Connections, an organization that empowers entrepreneurs, sales representatives, and professionals to become successful and gain more referrals through networking.

He is the author of several books, including Foundational Networking: Building Know, Like and Trust to Create a Lifetime of Extraordinary Success and The Three Reasons You Don't Get Referrals. See all his books and programs at frankagin.com.

Finally, Frank shares information and insights on professional relationships, business networking and best practices for generating referrals on the Networking Rx podcast.

In the summer of 2018, he started planning this short-form podcast. As he mapped out what he wanted to bring to an audience of entrepreneurs, sales representatives, and professionals, he knew he'd have hundreds of programs.

But in addition to all that content, Frank noticed he also had a plethora of other materials—instructive, insightful, and inspirational. All this additional content was worthwhile, but none of it was long enough to create a full episode of Networking Rx.

Not wanting the material to go to waste, Frank developed it into short essays—approximately 150 words each. Then he started to record and share those segments daily under the brand Networking Rx Minutes.

For years, he shared a daily message of empowerment, intuition, and hope. This is a compilation of 100 of those essays. Enjoy.

# -1-
# The Best Way From Point A to B

While the direct route usually appears to be the shortest route, in networking it is not always the best path. For example, you might be looking to meet Ms. "Big-Shot Decision Maker." Standing between you and her, however, (unfortunately) is an impressive gatekeeper system.

Don't be deterred. Rather commit to taking a circuitous route to your intended destination. Ask those in your trusty network for an introduction to someone who might know Ms. "Big-Shot Decision Maker." Or perhaps a connection to someone who might know someone who might know the ultimate target. Or maybe some insight as to where she might volunteer.

The point is that great contacts are not necessarily the easiest to get to, even though going from point A to B is shortest. Nevertheless, remember to use your network to help you connect. They can help you start at point A, land at point C (and then maybe work through D and E) to ultimately get you to point B.

## -2-
## The Strongest Relationships

In networking, you're encouraged to get people to like you. And that's certainly important. But being liked is not enough.

As corporate relationship consultant Bill Troy shares in his book *Clicksand: How Online Marketing Will Destroy Your Business*, "The strongest human bonds are not formed when two people like each other. Rather, the strongest relationships form when two people both like the same thing.

Troy refers to these as commonalities and remarks that they "can be anything from a similar sense of humor to a shared love of wine to having the same alma mater."

If you want the strongest possible relationship with someone, devote time and energy to finding commonalities. They're there. They might not be readily apparent. They might take time to uncover. But once you and someone you know uncover one or more commonalities, the speed at which the relationship solidifies will seem to accelerate. In no time, mere acquaintances can become lifelong friends.

# Acknowledgement

In sincere appreciation of Logan Agin.

This book (and this entire series) does not happen without the *Networking Rx* podcast.

And that podcast doesn't happen without you.

I am Groot!

# Table of Contents

## Look For These Other Books in This Series

*101 Essays to Empower You to Rise & Thrive*
*101 Essays to Empower You to Up Your Game*
*101 Essays to Empower You to Limitless Reach*
*101 Essays to Empower You to Elevate Your Influence*
*101 Essays to Empower You to Peak Performance*
*101 Essays to Empower You to The Winning Edge*
*101 Essays to Empower You to Live Unstoppable*
*101 Essays to Empower You to Achieve Greatness*
*101 Essays to Empower You to Break Barriers*

# Introduction

This book comes from the insight and creativity of Frank Agin.

Who is Frank? He is the founder and president of AmSpirit Business Connections, an organization that empowers entrepreneurs, sales representatives, and professionals to become successful and gain more referrals through networking.

He is the author of several books, including Foundational *Networking: Building Know, Like and Trust to Create a Lifetime of Extraordinary Success* and *The Three Reasons You Don't Get Referrals*. See all his books and programs at frankagin.com.

Finally, Frank shares information and insights on professional relationships, business networking and best practices for generating referrals on the Networking Rx podcast.

In the summer of 2018, he started planning this short-form podcast. As he mapped out what he wanted to bring to an audience of entrepreneurs, sales representatives, and professionals, he knew he'd have hundreds of programs.

But in addition to all that content, Frank noticed he also had a plethora of other materials—instructive, insightful, and inspirational. All this additional content was worthwhile, but none of it was long enough to create a full episode of Networking Rx.

Not wanting the material to go to waste, Frank developed it into short essays—approximately 150 words each. Then he started to record and share those segments daily under the brand Networking Rx Minutes.

For years, he shared a daily message of empowerment, intuition, and hope. This is a compilation of 100 of those essays. Enjoy.

# -1-
# Grow Like a Tree

Have you ever seen a fully-grown tree? No? Of course not. No one has. Why not? Because trees grow and grow until the day they die. As long as they are a live, they reach, expand and strive to be more than they are.

Be like that tree. Reach, expand and strive to be more than you are. Continue to grow your mind. Never stop learning. Be a perpetual student of knowledge.

You never know where that next great idea is going to come from. You never know what you might discover. You can't predict when a small tidbit of new information could change your world in a big way.

You do not have to enroll in night school or get another degree, but continue to read, attend seminars or programs, and listen to podcasts. Do whatever you can to keep your mind engaged. And commit to doing this until the day you die.

## -2-
## Move Beyond The Decision

Once upon a time there were three frogs sitting on a lily pad in a pond. Two frogs decided to jump in. How many frogs are left on the lily pad? The answer is three.

Is that a trick question? Hardly. You see, deciding to do something is not the same as doing it.

Yes, there are indecisive people. Those who can't decide whether to walk away from a situation or double down on it. And those who perpetually mull over a growing litany of options.

Equally bad, however, is the person who makes a decision but takes no action to see the decision through.

Don't be indecisive. Don't procrastinate. Determine your two or three best options. Assess the pros and cons of each. Then using this and trusting your gut, decide.

And, once you've decided, take a bold step in that direction. In other words, get your butt off that lily pad.

## -3-
## Build A Better World

Look around. No, the world is not perfect, including your corner of it.

Things are amiss in society. There are initiatives that are not hitting on all cylinders. And there are some that aren't functioning at all.

And there are things that are not only amiss, they're completely missing. There are underserved pieces of your community. There are programs that have disappeared. And there are programs that never were.

No, things are not perfect. But you have a choice. You can complain and rail about what's not. Or you can roll up your sleeves and become part of what will be. After all, sometimes you have to create that which you want to be part of.

So, if you want a better world around you, take a step today – no matter small it might be – to build your community into what you want it to be.

## -4-
## Challenge Equals Change

Try this: Walk 100 steps in any direction and then walk back. Can you feel the burn? Is your body sculpted? Of course not.

Now try this: Go to the library, pick up a business or leadership book and read the back cover. Are your business "smarts" appreciably improved for doing that? It's not likely.

Final exercise: Log onto social media (LinkedIn, Twitter, whatever) and 'like' a handful of posts. Is your network now teaming with loads of great, new relationships? Nope! No way.

These three exercises are meant to illustrate a point. If you want to change yourself, you need to challenge yourself. A healthy life needs you to invest more than a couple hundred steps. An improved business acumen requires real experience and consistent learning. Your network won't grow appreciably with only a few likes or shares.

The lesson is simple: If it doesn't challenge you, it's not going to change you.

# -5-
# Exit Conversations Gracefully

Making connections at networking events is great. Remember, however, that networking and these events in general, are about building relationships.

So, you want to become adept at having small talk conversations. But in addition, you need to become skillful at transitioning out of conversations so that you're able to move on to another.

Here are some great ideas on things to say to help you "gracefully exit" from one conversation so you can engage in another:

"Thanks for your time. I told myself I would meet three interesting people at this event. I have two more to go."

Or "Thanks for your time. There is someone over there that I need to connect with."

Or "Is there anyone here in particular you would like to meet? I would be glad to introduce you."

These statements are all useful in helping you transition from one great conversation to the next. So, keep these statements in your conversation arsenal.

## -6-
## Stand Tall

It's a long-standing Olympic tradition that during opening ceremonies each participating country selects a representative from its delegate of athletes to carry the nation's flag.

Each representative then carries its country's flag high and proud as they process around the venue. However, when they pass in front of the host nation's lead dignitary, they dip their flag in deference to that official and the host country.

Every country does this. Everyone ... except the United States.

You see, at the 1908 London Olympics, the United States flag bearer Ralph Rose refused to dip the American flag for King Edward VII. When questioned about it Rose proclaimed, "The American flag bows before no earthly king."

No doubt, you're great in your own right. Stand tall with pride. And like the American flag, don't bow before anyone on this earth.

# -7-
# The Fifth Habit

In Stephen Covey's renowned book, *The 7 Habits of Highly Effective People*, he advocates that for us to have the best possible relationships, we need to start by employing empathetic listening skills. That is, we should be listening with the intent to understand as opposed to listening with the intent to reply.

Through listening to understand, we place ourselves in someone else's shoes. We see the world through their eyes. And, as best we can, we understand their way of thinking. In essence, through the level of listening that Covey promotes we achieve the capacity to understand or feel what another person is experiencing.

Certainly, with this level of understanding, we better position ourselves to serve them, which is important. But an added benefit is that by engaging in this empathetic listening we increase the likelihood that people will listen to us with the intent to understand.

# -8-
# Crucial Conversations

No matter who you are or what you do, you can't avoid an occasional interaction that you sense will be, well, tense, contentious or generally uncomfortable. In these moments, your gut gives you two options: prepare for battle or run and hide.

However, according to authors of the book *Crucial Conversations* there is a third option. When communication is headed towards conflict, these authors encourage you to ask yourself three questions:

One, what do you want for this person?
Two, what do you want for yourself?
And, three, what do you want for the relationship?

The benefit of reflecting on these questions is that this line of thinking pulls your brain out of the primitive "fight or flight" mindset and engages a higher order of consideration. That alone will soften tensions and get you in the right frame of mind to empower a more productive result.

## -9-

## Was That Networking Event Worthwhile?

Here are questions you likely ponder after most any networking event are: Was it worth the trip? What it worth the time spent mingling? Are the contacts I made worth anything? Was that event worthwhile?

Know this: In reality, the answers to these questions are always a resounding "Absolutely!"

Think about it: Every event offers value. Yes, some events offer more value than others. They all have value, however.

And, yes, the value from some events is more immediate, while the true value of others takes time to develop and fully present itself.

So, certainly assess the value of events as best you can. And certainly, track your results however you deem appropriate.

But before you completely pass judgment on an event, remember this: The benefits of any networking activity may not present themselves for weeks, months, or even years. So be patient. Keep attending those events.

## -10-
## The Second Arrow

A Buddhist monk once shared with his students, "If a person is struck by an arrow, it is painful. But it is the second arrow that is even more painful."

He went on to explain that the first arrow represents all the the bad things that might happen to you in life.

The second arrow, however, represents all your negative reactions to the first. For example, if you needlessly blame others for the first arrow or become overly critical of yourself, in a sense you inflict yourself with added pain. And this added pain generally is much more hurtful than that from the first arrow.

In life, bad things are going to happen. Some are your fault, and some are not. Blaming others won't take away the sting of the setback. So why do it? And beating yourself up over it takes energy away from moving forward.

So, endure life's first arrows, but avoid the second ones at all costs.

# -11-
# Shut Up and Listen

Award winning business coach, motivational speaker, and author of A Life Best Lived: A Story of Life, Death and Second Chances, Danny Creed has some sage advice for achieving your goals and dreams: Simply serve others around you. Your family. Your friends. Your clients. Your colleagues. Your vendors.

This then begs the question, "How do I best serve others?" He has great advice for that too. It's simply this: SHUT UP AND LISTEN.

When you do that, you can help others be successful by understanding their own definition of success. To effectively listen, you need to completely focus your attention on the person and be genuinely interested, with an intent to actually learn.

Moreover, don't interrupt. Don't argue. Stay off e-mail, text and social media. And, by all mean, lean into the conversation with your body and eye contact.

Coach Creed is right. Success starts by serving others. And serving others starts by shutting up and listening.

## -12-
## The Reconnection Call

If you're like most, your life is littered with relationships with whom you've lost touch. No one is to blame. These things happen. For whatever reason, their life and yours have taken different paths.

And while, you may no longer be on the same life path, there is still tremendous value in these contacts. So, you should make an opportunity from time to time to simply reconnect. But how?

Donna Fisher, in her book *People Power*, has some straightforward advice: Simply call. Labeling this a "Reconnection Call", Fisher indicates that it is made for the purpose of "re-establishing a relationship."

Once we have the person on the line, simply acknowledge that it has been a long time, and then express an interest in catching up. Although it may feel awkward at first, remember your old friend is being reconnected too. So, your call will be a welcome benefit to him or her as well.

## -13-
## Trees & Grass

Twentieth-century author Hal Borland once said, "Knowing trees, I understand the meaning of patience. Knowing grass, I can appreciate persistence."

Be like a tree. You can't expect to be at your peak potential overnight. Rather, like a tree, you break through as merely a seedling in your chosen field of expertise. Then year after year, you reach and grow, expanding bit by bit. And all along, capitalizing on opportunities to take in the enlightenment of knowledge and experience.

But also, be like grass. You will endure setbacks, figuratively being stepped on and cut down. Whatever the case, just keep going. Be undeterred by challenges. Overcome and continue on. Let no one stop you from achieving what you're hardwired to achieve.

When things don't move at the pace you'd like, look up and remember the trees. Adopt their patience. When you encounter that setback, look down at the grass. Take a lesson from it and relentlessly persist.

## -14-
## Bonnie Richardson High

In 2009, Rochelle High School won the Texas Class 1A high school girls track and field championship for the second year in a row. No big deal, right? Someone wins the championship every year. And, from time to time a high school will do it back-to-back.

What made this title unique, however, was that while state track championships are generally a team effort, these championships were the result of one girl's effort – Bonnie Richardson.

Yes, this one young woman, competing against teams with multiple athletes, did enough to single-handedly win a state track and field championship. She won the high jump. Placed second in the long jump. Finished third in the discus. Won the 200 meter. And took second in the 100 meter.

Life can be like this. Sometimes you don't have a team to rely upon. Sometimes, if you really want to succeed, it's just up to you.

# -15-
# Rainmaker Contacts

It is great to be connected to people who want what you sell here and now. It can, however, be more lucrative long-term to build your network with contacts who can connect you to these clients on a consistent basis.

These are rainmaker contacts, and they are vital to ongoing success. Who are they? These are entrepreneurs or professionals who don't do what you do, but their clientele is virtually identical to yours. For example, a business banker would benefit from meeting a CPA type, as these accountant types can refer their clients.

With this understanding, do three things. One, identify who are the potential rainmaker contacts in your world. Next, find opportunities to interact with these entrepreneurs and professionals. Then, finally, from time to time ask your network to introduce you to them.

These are three important steps as rainmaker contacts represent a treasure trove of new business.

## -16-
## Adhere To the Golden Rule

Do you want more from your network? Of course, you do. You're not alone. Everyone does.

Everyone wants more referrals. Everyone wants to be connected to more opportunities. Everyone seeks inroads to great, game-changing information. And everyone wants all the other benefits that a network can provide. So, like everyone else, you want more from your network.

What most people fails to realize, however, is that if you want to get more from your network you need to focus on giving more to it. Though this might seem completely counterintuitive, it's true.

This is often referred to as the Golden Rule of Networking and is simply stated as "Give First; Get Second." This law is universal and is rooted in human nature, spanning time and remaining consistent from one culture to another.

So, if you want more from your network, begin today infusing it with referrals, opportunities, contacts, energy and whatever else could help others. In time, this will come back to you in plenty.

## -17-
## Energy Follows Focus

On the July 5th, 2019 episode of the *How To Be Mesmerizing* podcast, host Tim Shurr reminded his audience that the path they're on (even though it might be fraught with difficulty) is the path they're supposed to be on.

As for dealing with life's trials and tribulations, Shurr offered this advice:

When facing a challenging situation, whatever it might be, take a step back and do what you can to ignore the challenge itself. Instead, in that moment, ask yourself what outcome you really want.

In this same spirit, he encouraged his audience not to commiserate about where they are in life. Rather, he advocated that they think about and get a clear picture as to who they wanted to be.

Keep your eye on the positive. Zero in on a vision of hope and promise.

Shurr's point is simple. Where your focus goes, your energy follows.

# -18-
# Don't Misrepresent Yourself

It is said that to conceal a single lie, it takes at least 15 other lies. And then to conceal each of those 15 lies, you'll need a whopping 225 more lies just to conceal one single incident of deceit. And from there … well, you get the picture.

It takes far more time and energy to conceal a falsehood than it does to simply own up to and deal with the truth.

Be honest in all matters, even as it relates to your personal brand. You know in your heart of hearts when effective marketing or spin crosses the line into outright misrepresentation. So, you're best to stay well on the right side and away from the gray area.

This is the reality: eventually an exaggeration "gone-too-far" will come back to haunt you. This moment could then quickly destroy any and all credibility you you've worked so hard to build.

So be honest. Don't misrepresent yourself.

## -19-
## The Attractiveness of Courage

Life is not an endless succession of forward progress. While you may enjoy success, at some point or another you will also encounter frustrating challenges and disappointing setbacks. It is during these moments of hardship that you have the greatest opportunity to establish your personal brand and build your network.

You see, when you stare down frustrating challenges and disappointing setbacks with an attitude of determination, you establish yourself as courageous. This draws others toward you.

There is little question that people love an underdog. And they can't help but rally around one who is battling to overcome some sort of setback or hardship. So, by demonstrating an attitude of courageous determination, others want to draw from this strength, and they hope to take inspiration from it. In any event, they cannot help but want to get to know you better and cannot help but want to get to like you more.

## -20-
## If You Pledge To, Do So

As you interact with others, it's only a matter of time before you make a gratuitous commitment to someone. It's only a matter of time before you agree to fulfil a request someone's made. It might be to share information. It might be to make an introduction. It might be to arrange a meeting at a later day and time.

Whatever the situation, however you've promised to follow through, do so.

Remember, successful networking is about building relationships where others come to know, like and trust you. As such, a key component to the element of trust is being reliable. And inherent in reliability is doing what you say you will.

By not doing so – whether you fail to deliver or simply never were able to – the end result is the same. You impair networking potential by hurting your relationships. So, if you pledge to do something, make sure you do it.

# -21-
# FROG Questioning

In his book, *The Seven Levels of Communication: Go from Relationships to Referrals*, author Michael Maher encourages through the edification of his protagonists that to build your network most effectively, you should build a FROG into your conversations.

Yes, FROG. F, R, O, G. It's an acronym to remind you to focus on the other person and help guide your questioning to encompass four things:

One, F, Family: Inquire about their family situation. Married. Single. Children. Where they're from.

Two, R, Recreation: Ask questions that serve to get people talking about their interests and passions. Hobbies. Favorite sports and teams. Volunteer endeavors.

Three, O, Occupation: Be sure to get the person talking about their professional life. Not just what they do, but also how they got started in that.

And, finally, G, for Goals: Inquire as to their goals, hopes, dreams and aspirations.

As Maher implies, the first step to being well known is knowing others first.

# -22-
# The Value of Curiosity

Kay Coughlin, CEO at Facilitator on Fire, shares that there is value to curiosity.

Certain things thrive in a curious world. Things like science, fruitful debate, growth, tolerance, delight in the unknown, and forgiveness.

She also shares that unfortunately other things thrive in a polarized, only-one-right-answer world. Things like insecurity, small mindset, fear of the unknown, extreme politics, hate, bigotry, blame, and shame.

With that, Kay encourages that instead of, "I'm right, you're wrong," ask "How could this be different or improved?"

And rather than, "This isn't what I asked for," try, "I didn't expect this, please tell me more."

Her message is crystal clear: Insecure people can't tolerate curiosity. So, strive to be secure enough to be curious. This will help you be a better leader. It will help you build a stronger team. It will ensure that your network thrives.

# -23-
# Speak Slowly

In his book, *The 100 Simple Secrets of Successful People*, Dr. David Niven shared the results of a 1995 study on speech rate. It concluded that individuals "rate speakers who talk more slowly as being 38 percent more knowledgeable than speakers who talk more quickly."

Assuming this and knowing that it is generally better for you to be considered more knowledgeable, here are some suggestions for controlling the pace at which you speak:

First, from time to time, review in your own mind what you generally have to say.

Second, start any conversation or program by building a little rapport with those you're talking to.

Third, remind yourself that in most situations, you are the expert. Relax. Share what you know best.

Finally, take a couple deep breaths every so often as you talk. This will naturally relax you.

These simple guidelines will make you more effective at speaking slowly and, as a result, will add more value to what you have to say.

# -24-
# Don't Wing It

Sure, there are people who can come up with an answer seemingly on the fly and get away with it. And perhaps you were great in high school and college at BS-ing your way through that esoteric class where much of the grade depended upon class participation.

But none of that works in the real world. This is the reality: the people around you are smart. They might not let on that they know when you're "going off the cuff" but they know. And while it might not be readily apparent, this seemingly innocent maneuver is read as a deception by others. As such, it serves to undermine the integrity you're working hard to build.

So, endeavor to be as prepared as possible. When asked about something, share what you can. And when there is something about which you're unclear, don't wing it. Respect their intelligence and save your integrity. Simply indicate that you don't know the answer, but you'd be happy to look into it.

# -25-
# Bridge The Gap

Stop and think! There is likely someone you'd love to be introduced to. Maybe it's someone in your area. Maybe it's someone in another region of the country. Maybe it's someone on LinkedIn. Whatever the case, it's someone you'd like to meet.

But you don't know them. And while you're not shy, it can seem a little ... well ... awkward reaching out to a complete stranger and suggesting "Hey, let's get acquainted."

If this describes you, here is a simple, but effective strategy for becoming connected and avoiding all the potential awkwardness: Consider having another person act as a go–between for you.

Simply find someone in your network who is already connected to the person you'd like to meet and ask them to introduce you. They can do it easily via LinkedIn. They can connect you two via e-mail. Or if it makes sense, they could set up a face-to-face meeting.

Whatever the case, utilize a mutual connection to bridge the gap.

## -26-
## Inroads To Thought Leadership

Do you like to stand before a group and share insight and knowledge on your industry or profession? Would you be comfortable writing a similar article or piece for a newsletter?

If the answer is "YES," from time to time remind your network that a good opportunity for you is an introduction to a group or organization that might be interested in a professional program on your expertise.

Chances are, in your area there are groups and organizations that would truly find value in what you have to say. In so doing, you brand yourself as a subject-matter expert as well as grow your network amongst lots of potential clients (and people who know potential clients).

While this sort of activity may not generate immediate business, it will absolutely build a foundation upon which lots of future business can result.

# -27-
# Light Someone's Candle

Bob Graham, corporate trainer, speaker and author of the book *Breakthrough Communication Skills*, points out that a single person with a lit candle can, in mere seconds, be the catalyst for lighting an entire room of candles by simply sharing the light.

Graham's point is simple: Metaphorically, we all hold a lit candle. Within each of us is a burning inspiration and flames of motivation.

And yet at the same time, we're all surrounded by a litany of others whose candles are unlit. Their spirits are indifferent, dejected, or bordering on being completely demoralized.

With very little effort, we can use our passion to ignite the spirits of these listless souls. From there, the light will spread to others. And the best part is that sharing this does nothing to diminish the light within us.

So, take a moment today and light someone's candle. Then watch as that flame fans out to others.

## -28-
## The Seeds Of Altruism

To build a network you need to give to others, which isn't always easy. But the starting point for giving to others is being thoughtful. You know, being considerate of the feelings of others (whether you know them or not) and finding ways you can have a positive impact on their lives.

In his book, *Winning Without Intimidation*, Bob Burg indicates that while being thoughtful does not always come naturally, it's a simple idea that requires no incredible skills.

Burg maintains that being thoughtful is nothing more than a habit and encompasses such occasional and basic acts as:

Holding a door open for someone.
Paying someone a well-deserved compliment.
Parking a bit farther from the entrance.

Each of these is simple and represents only a tiny portion of an almost endless list of thoughtful acts. If you focus on being thoughtful towards others, eventually it becomes a habit. From there, giving more to others will quickly follow.

# -29-
# Got Lunch?

Relationships are not easy. Yes, understanding a general notion of what you should and shouldn't do is easy. Executing in real time, however, is often very difficult, right?

Afterall, everything is in a state of flux. Situations constantly change. Wants and needs change. Moods change. And that's just you. These same things are happening to the people with whom you're interacting. And none of this is choreographed at all.

Thinking about all of that, it's no wonder that your relationships seem to get off-track from time to time. Right?

When it happens, this one simple thing will help: Lunch. Yep, lunch. Here's the reality. It's nearly impossible to hold ill will toward someone with whom you are sharing a meal.

So, if your relationship with someone is strained, invite them to lunch. This might not fix everything, but it will start the process ... and fill your belly at the same time.

## -30-
## The Knight in Shining Armor

Do you know what most people hope for? A knight in shining armor. They quietly and desperately hope that somebody comes riding in and rescues them from a less-than-fulfilling existence. Or ensures that their dreams and aspirations are realized. Or at a minimum, feeds them all sorts of great referrals, information, and business contacts.

But here is a thought:  Rather than looking for the Knight In Shining Armor, why not become the Knight In Shining Armor ... focusing your energies on helping others. Think about it.

When you do, you become unique and special in any setting. And as everyone else is looking for a Knight In Shining Armor, they are in reality looking and wanting to meet you. Sounds neat, huh?

Plus, as you serve your role as the Knight In Shining Armor (providing referrals, information and contacts), you inspire others to want to give back to you. Thus, in the end, your service to others, serves to help you.

# -31-
# Tiny Billboards

According to Susan RoAne, author of *How To Work A Room: The Ultimate Guide To Making Lasting Connections In Person and Online*:

"The purpose of business cards is to give people a tangible, physical way to remember you."

In a sense, your business cards serve to brand you, just like a billboard brands a business or product. After all, it's completely pointless to meet others unless you are committed to having them remember you. Right? This begs a series of questions for you to consider:

What does your business card tell others about you? Is it something worth remembering? And is that information presented in a manner that's easy to understand?

Assuming your business card is a great and memorable representation of you, then answer this: Do you always have clean, crisp business cards to distribute? In your pocket? In your portfolio? In your car?

As you prepare to venture out today, ensure that you've got a great business card and plenty of them.

# -32-
# The Exploration of Networking

Networking is simply human interaction, and it has been with us since the beginning of recorded time. These human interactions are really just the relationships we have with one another. Some connections are passing. Some connections are more lasting. Some connections are seemingly lifelong.

Given this, networking is, more or less, really just human behavior. Talking. Listening. Understanding. Being empathetic, encouraging, inspiring, smiling, laughing, and being a friend.

The wonderful thing about human behavior is that there are patterns to it. While the patterns may not be perfectly predictable, there are patterns there.

When there are patterns, there is curiosity. And when there is curiosity, you will find people of science trying to explain the patterns through studying, observing, and examining them.

Know this, relationships are no different. For years, the social sciences have examined how humans relate to one another. Embrace this curiosity.

## -33-
## Networking – A Great Adventure

In his book *Three New People: Make the Most of Your Daily Interactions and Stop Missing Amazing Opportunities,* author Brian Miller makes this powerful statement: "You have no idea what kind of opportunities await you just on the other side of the next connection."

It's true. New connections lead to an adventure of wonder.

Yes, new connections introduce you to a whole new roster of people that then open doors to places and things you never knew existed.

No doubt, new connections also become dynamic colleagues who serve to enhance your abilities and expand your vision of what's possible for you professionally.

And, of course, these new connections become wonderful friends creating a new level of laughter, support and happiness in your life.

Yes, beyond that first handshake with someone new is an awesome journey of amazement and wonder. You just need to make the effort to embark on the adventure.

# -34-
# Compare Lists and Networks

When you work with your customers or clients, chances are you are completely focused on them. And you should be. That is how you provide impeccable service.

The problem is that in this intentional focus, you may overlook opportunities to refer or introduce others in your network. No problem, though.

To uncover these potential missed opportunities, take time periodically to compare your list of clients to those in your network that you interact with on a consistent basis. In that quiet moment, reflect upon your interaction with your clients. Perhaps they said something that might be an opportunity for a networking contact. Or perhaps there is someone in your network your client could benefit from meeting.

While this will not always happen, from time to time an opportunity or two will materialize. Those will add up over time. And these will serve to endear you more to your network.

# -35-
# Dare Mighty Things

In 1899, before he was President of the United States, Teddy Roosevelt said to a group in Chicago, Illinois:

"Far better is it to dare mighty things, to win glorious triumphs, even though checkered by failure... than to rank with those poor spirits who neither enjoy nor suffer much, because they live in a gray twilight that knows not victory nor defeat."

Over 120 years later, Roosevelt's words still ring true. Success is not necessarily about winning. It's about putting oneself out there. It's about taking the chance. It's about being bold.

Go to that event you've never been to before. Reach out and introduce yourself to that business icon and see where the conversation goes. Publish that article or book. Volunteer to head up that committee at work or in your community.

Yes, some of these things won't work out. What of it? You were bold and dared a mighty thing. That alone is worth something.

## -36-
## Be a Quarterback

A powerful means of generating referrals for others in your ongoing networking circles is to communicate to your family, friends, customers, and clients something like the following:

> "Hey, to let you know, I have a working relationship with dozens of individuals representing various businesses and professions. I consider these individuals as trusted colleagues that aid me in the service of people like you. Therefore, if you are ever in need of a product or service and you are not certain who to contact, please contact me. I would be happy to assist you in locating the appropriate business or profession."

However, you choose to communicate this, it will position you as a "Go To" person amongst your network, and they will come to you for help. While you will be coming to their assistance, you will also benefit your networking partners in the process – which will further endear you to them.

## -37-
## Cooperation Understood

Wouldn't it be great if we all agreed on everything? If we all said yes and moved in lock step in the same direction? It would be great. But that's not how it is.

Everyone is different. We all move at a different pace. We all have varying hopes, dreams, and aspirations. Yet, we all need to cooperate.

Understand, however, that cooperation doesn't mean agreement, per se. It does, however, mean working together to advance the greater good. So, as you interact with others, be respectful enough to allow them to share. Be mindful enough to try to understand what they are trying to convey.

None of this suggests that you need to capitulate to anyone else's position. It simply means that you should be open to the notion that other opinions exist. And being open to hearing and understanding other opinions might help you find a middle ground that serves everyone.

# -38-
# Course Correct

A plane takes off from London heading to New York. If it is nudged off course by just five degrees to the south, it will end up landing somewhere south of Mexico, in like Venezuela or Belize. That's crazy. It ends up approximately 2,500 miles from its intended destination.

This is why pilots continually check the heading of the flight and, as needed, make necessary course corrections.

The same is true with your life. It's great to have a clear vision, reasonable goals and a committed plan of action. But from time to time, it's also important to look up to check that you're still pointed in the right direction.

After all, things change. Situations change. Your own wants and needs change. The people around you change. It's all subject to change. And all of it impacts your route. So, to ensure that you are headed where you intended to go, remember to course correct whenever necessary.

# -39-
# Leaders Lead

Leaders lead. They don't seek permission. They lead.

They don't wait to be elected. They lead.

They don't wait to be asked. They lead.

They're the first to arrive. The last to leave. They roll up their sleeves and dig into whatever they're asking of others. And they don't stop until they ensure all is done.

Leaders lead without title, compensation or recognition. Leaders lead to fill a void of courage. Leaders lead to create a vision that's not quite clear. Leaders lead to offer care and empathy when they see the need. Leaders lead.

Here is the reality: You're a leader. It might be of a vast, far flung corporate empire. Or it might be a certain aspect of a small group or team. It might just be a younger someone needing that guiding mindset.

Wherever. Whomever. However. You're a leader. Embrace that role with pride. Throwback your shoulders. Lift your chin up high. And always remember, leaders lead.

## -40-
## Sledding Through Life

No doubt, you aspire to have your life proceed like an afternoon of sledding on a snow-covered hill. You seek to position yourself so that you effortlessly glide along at a pace so exhilarating that the wind seems to blow through your hair.

The fact of the matter is that your life is much like a day of sledding. The problem is, however, that you need to remember that a big part of sledding – and life – is trudging uphill with a sled in tow.

In sledding, while the uphill hike is tedious, hard work and even boring, the effort of the ascent puts you in position to take the ride. Life is no different. Every period of seemingly effortless achievement has been preceded by some degree of toil and drudgery.

In summary, in both sledding and life, to enjoy the ride you must take an uphill hike first.

# -41-
# Hold Your Fire

Imagine this: You're at an event, standing with someone new. Someone great. Someone you've longed to connect with. And before long, you're engaged headlong in conversation. In fact, you've done well. You've got them talking. Awesome, right?

But then, in your excitement, before they finish, you interject, cutting them off. UGH! This is not only potentially embarrassing, but your conversation partner might perceive that you aren't terribly interested in listening. And you don't want that.

Consciously focus on what the other person is saying. Hear them out. Do not jump to conclusions about what is being said. Listen for details or clues as to where they might like the conversation to go.

Then, take a deep breath. Yes, take an actual deep breath before you respond. A second of silence won't kill the conversation. Rather, that brief moment will allow you to have a better response, which will lead to a better conversation and the perception that you're truly listening. This serves to build the relationship.

## -42-
## Acting On Common Sense

The world has plenty of smart people. But sadly, many of those smart people don't reach their potential. Why? It's not lack of desire. It's not a deficiency of hard work. It's not a matter of poor luck.

No. It comes down to common sense or a lack thereof.

You see, ten percent of reaching your potential is knowing your business or trade well. The other 90 percent comes down to executing on common sense.

Little things. Overlooked things. Seemingly invisible things. Things like, being on time. Following up. Saying thank you. And a couple dozen other things that you'd call common sense.

Yes, these are common sense. And you might dismiss them for that reason. But the reality is that they aren't necessarily common practice. And that's the separator between mediocrity and lasting success.

So be smart. Reach your potential. Remember to execute on common sense often.

## -43-
## Be Proud and Step Closer

Major League Soccer goalkeeper Jon Kempin, of the Columbus Crew, shared on his Twitter feed, "Before you go to sleep, remember all the beautiful victories you had today. Be proud of yourself because tomorrow you're one step closer to where you want to be."

Kempin's words have a broad application and any and everyone should embrace this wisdom. Whether you're an athlete or not, every day you experience victories. You conquer a fear. You learn a skill. You complete something lingering on your list.

Each of these victories builds on the ones from the day before, which have built on the ones before that. And so on. Each of these victories slowly moves you forward. Day after day. Week after week until, in time, you've accomplished something significant. That advanced degree. A successful business. Perhaps a notable podcast.

And it all relates back to the beautiful victories you had today. So, close your eyes and gets some rest. And be very, very proud.

## -44-
## Returns On Networking Investments

Know this, everything you do with respect to your network will somehow, some way, come back to you. Referrals given work into referrals for you in return. Encouragement comes back as encouragement. Introductions made result in introductions received. Know that what you put into your network comes back to you.

With that, also know this. Very little (if any) of what you do for your network will come back to you tomorrow. Or even next week. Or, perhaps next month, for that matter. You simply need to trust that what you put into your network will eventually come back to you.

So, while you wait for these returns on your networking investment, remain optimistic about your networking efforts and simply keep contributing. And as you do, do whatever you can to keep from being discouraged. You've made an investment. The returns are coming. Believe that.

# -45-
# Weak Ties Are Strong Ones

Sociological research has shown that the vast majority of opportunities your network provides will not come from close ties, such as friends and relatives. Rather great career opportunities, new client wins, and groundbreaking information come from weak ties. These are people you know, but ones that you only see and interact with occasionally.

Why? Because close ties tend to occupy the same world as you do. Think about it. A spouse or close friend may share many of the same network contacts you already know.

Mere acquaintances, or "weak ties", on the other hand, are much more likely to know people that you do not. While you might share a small overlap in networks, most of the people they know are completely unknown to you.

So, when it comes to job hunting or finding clients or generally getting ahead, there is much strength in connecting with weak ties.

## -46-
## The Two-Way Street

Michael Goldberg, author of *Knockout Networking* has a saying: "Networking is a two-way street!"

To elaborate, he then suggests a litany of questions to ponder in any relationship:

How can we help one another?
How can we work together?
How can we be resources for one another?
How can we refer each other?

These are great questions. And ones that you shouldn't consider rhetorical. Rather, whenever you're in conversation with someone else ... whenever you're thinking about contacts in your network ... whenever you're looking to add value to others .... you should take an active approach to finding reasonable answers to these questions.

As Goldberg will tell you, effective networking is an ongoing process of learning about others and then finding ways to help them. If you consistently engage in this thought process, the vast majority of the time you'll uncover things you can do to help others. And once you're consistently helping other, in time, things will come back to you.

# -47-
# Brick Walls

What you do, whatever it is, isn't easy, right? If you're like most people it can seem like life conspires against you, and what should be simple gets complicated in a hurry. It can feel as though the "gremlins" of life have put obstacles in your way that prevent you from doing what you intend to do.

When you encounter these roadblocks, heed the advice of Dr. Randy Pausch. A computer professor at Carnegie Melon University, Pausch made an inspiring "last lecture" months before succumbing to terminal brain cancer in the fall of 2007. Pausch called these obstacles brick walls. He believed that brick walls are not there to prevent you from doing the things you want or hope to do. Rather, brick walls are there to simply assess how bad you want it.

So, the next time you face a roadblock or obstacle, don't commiserate. Rather remind yourself of exactly how much you want what you're after.

# -48-
# Set An Example of Action

Networking is a verb, an action word. Thus, you cannot network by sitting back and letting the world operate around you. You need to get out there and actively involve yourself.

At work, if there are extracurricular projects to tackle or committees on which to serve, be at the forefront of getting involved. In your business, take the initiative of finding an industry association to join. In addition to your work or business, actively involve yourself with local school, civic and charitable organizations.

What is so special about you being actively involved? Like magic, it transforms you into something special. People want to associate with you when you are actively engaged in something beyond the daily minimum requirements.

When you set an example of action, you project yourself as a doer and a person with achievement potential. And these prospects of success attract others to you. Your action gives others a much greater interest in getting to know, like and trust you.

## -49-
## Opportunities For Revenue

Adam Connors, speaker, social architect, and founder of NetworkWise, is fond of saying that "Relationships are opportunities for revenue." In short, Connors implies that from relationships comes revenue.

No, a relationship is not a guarantee of revenue. And some are not intended to be revenue-generating. But revenue seldom comes without some form of relationship. Sure, people might order books, flowers, or dog food over the phone or online. But serious purchases and long-time clients, well, they are all born out of the relationships that Connors is referring to.

Remember, the people who do business with you and the people who associate with you, do so because they have some level of relationship with you. Over time, you've done things to help them know, like and trust you.

So, if you're looking to build revenue, double down on the one thing that creates opportunities for it. Invest time and attention to your relationships.

# -50-
## Focus on What You Can Control

Let's face it. Everyone's life is full of uncertainty. There is no guarantee of business, employment, or income. Any or all of that can be gone tomorrow.

Additionally, no one can say how their health will hold. Illness or worse can come out of nowhere. And every day, you're getting a little older, increasing the likelihood.

And you can't control the growth or dimension of your connections. People move. They retire. Allegiances change. Your network is prone to shift. That's just life.

In short, you cannot be sure as to how anything will turn out. All you can do is double down on the things you can control. And all you can really control is your mindset and the effort you put forth.

So, work hard at whatever you aspire to and maintain a hopeful and positive attitude as you do. Focus on these things and then just let the chips fall where they may.

## -51-
## The Four Oxen and The Lion

One of Aesop's Fables goes like this: A Lion prowled about a field in which four oxen dwelled. Many a time the lion tried to attack the oxen but whenever he approached, they would turn their tails to one another. So that whichever way the lion approached, he was challenged by a set of large and threatening horns. He had no hope in taking down any of the oxen.

Then one day, the oxen began quarreling amongst themselves. Frustrated with each other, they went off to graze alone in separate corners of the field. With this change, the Lion attacked them one by one and soon brought an end to all four.

Your network is much like the four oxen working in unity. When figuratively shoulder to shoulder with those you know, like and trust, you (and they) become more formidable than when you attempt to take on the world alone.

Remember: United you stand, divided you fall.

## -52-
## Contact Classification, Easy As 1-2-3-4

In his book, *Who Do You Want To Meet*, author Rob Thomas offers a simple way to classify your network. The purpose of this is to ensure that you make the highest and best use of your time in cultivating relationships: Start by rating your list of contacts on a scale one to four.

Ones are individuals with whom you are newly connected.

Twos are people you know. But these are people who you've had no real contact with for some time. The relationship is there, but it's dormant until one of you takes action.

Threes are those connections where there is an active relationship, but the benefits are generally one sided. Either you're doing things for them and them not reciprocating or vice versa. And...

Fours are those relationships that are mutually beneficial.

With this classification in hand, you'll know best how to invest time and energy in your relationships. Plus, you'll have a great understanding of how you can work to improve your network.

## -53-
## Be Genuinely Happy for Others

This world has more than its share of envy and jealousy. None of this serves anyone. So, resist those feelings as they simply position you with the masses.

Rather, be extraordinary. Find it in your heart to be truly happy for others.

If someone gets a raise or promotion, become giddy for them as if it were your own.

When they get that great house, the one even better than yours, smile for them as they no doubt earned it.

When they find true love, share in their joy and let it warm your soul too.

After all, envy and jealousy will rob you of vital energy. But sharing in the joy of others will serve to lift you and stoke your passion.

Remember, the good fortune of others doesn't diminish your opportunity for it. Rather it provides a beacon of hope that goodness is out there for you too.

# -54-
# Ripples of Goodness

Think of where you are in life right now. Okay, it's not perfect. No one's life is. But if you're honest, you'll admit, it's pretty darn good.

And sure, you've worked hard, made smart moves and had a bit of luck. But much of the goodness you enjoy has been created by others. Somewhere in the past, the efforts and sacrifices of people you may or may not know have rippled forward to serve you. Creating opportunities. Establishing programs. Clearing a figurative path.

Now it's your turn. It's your turn to put forth effort and make sacrifice to benefit others.

Serve your family.
Serve your neighbors.
Serve your community.

It's your turn to create your own ripples of goodness. Creating opportunities. Establishing programs. Clearing a figurative path. Know this: The good you do today never dies. It rolls forward. It lives on. In other people, in other places and throughout time. Your good deeds live on forever.

# -55-
# You, The CEO

On the August 26th, 2019 episode of the *How To Be Mesmerizing Podcast*, host Tim Shurr got his guest Duane Cummins, a corporate chief executive and author, to share his thoughts on the true meaning of being a CEO.

Cummins quickly remarked that CEO really stands for Constantly Elevating Others. In short, he explained that the role of any leader is to raise up those under his or her care. And being a leader is about serving others and not about being served.

In this sense, whoever you are, you are a CEO. It might not be of a far-flung corporate enterprise. It might only be of a single person, but you are charged with ensuring that someone is elevated. Someone is developed. Someone is nurtured. Someone is better today than they were yesterday.

It doesn't matter what your LinkedIn profile or business card says. You're a CEO. Lean into that role and elevate others.

# -56-
# Standing O-H ... I-O

Towards the end of the 1940 Michigan-Ohio State football game, Buckeye fans in attendance at Ohio Stadium made a standing ovation. That is not uncommon for a football program such as the Ohio State University. It's an enthusiastic crowd and they often show their appreciation for a great performance.

This particular ovation, however, was for the opponent's star player. You see, Michigan's Tom Harmon almost single-handedly delivered a 40 to nothing loss on the Buckeyes.

No doubt you have competitors. Some of them might even rise to the level of being rivals. Great. If done the right way, this is healthy, as it serves to make you better and it collectively heightens the level of service in the entire business community.

In summary, great people applaud the achievement of others, even if they are competitors. So, when you see or learn of a remarkable performance in your professional world, don't be afraid to let the person know. Recognizing them serves to make you a great person too.

## -57-
## The Hunchback Prince

Centuries ago, a kingdom had a prince with a hunchback. Though it was his destiny to be king, he was so tragically deformed that even the most loyal of subjects dreaded the day he would ascend to the throne.

Undeterred, the Prince ordered the royal sculptor to carve a statue of him in a manner that looked exactly as he would look if he had no deformity.

When the sculpture was finished, the Prince would approach it each day and try to bend his back straight up against the back of his statue. Then one day, bending upward, his shoulders touched the statute. He now resembled the statue he'd ordered constructed.

Your life today is riddled with imperfection and deformities relative to where you want to take it. In your mind, carve a statute of your perfect future self. Then each day bend a little more towards it. Like the Prince, one day your imperfections will be cast aside.

## -58-
## Be Grateful

In the book *Be Connected: Strategies To Attract The Right Opportunities, Connections And Clients Through Effective Networking*, consultant, speaker, and author Terry Bean writes:

"Being grateful for what you have is far more powerful than complaining about what you lack."

He goes on to explain that maintaining an attitude of gratitude allows you to have the right mindset. It's from this proper attitude that you actually attract more of what you seek.

The human mind focuses on and becomes attuned to situations in your mind. If you dwell on life's imperfections (and we all have them), you'll find more and more of them. And, in time, become consumed by a downward spiral of negativity.

But if you focus on and become grateful for whatever you have, your brain will work to attract more of it. Be thankful for all the wonderful things in life ... personal and professional ... and you'll find that additional goodness will come your way.

# -59-
# Own Your Failures

If you've been at this game of business long enough you will no doubt experience failures and setbacks. Some will be relatively small, such as not upselling a client at the 11th hour on the last day of an already record month. Others will be large, such as not getting the promotion or losing that big client. And a good many will be somewhere in between.

Whatever the case, these moments will leave you feeling a degree of disappointment. And that's okay, as that's part of being driven and goal oriented. What's not okay, however, is blaming others or circumstances as you ruminate on your shortcoming.

Whatever the "would have's", "should have's" and "could have's" might be, in the final analysis on some level it's your failure. Own it. Commit to doing better. Then move forward with your pride and the respect of others.

## -60-
## Airplane Maintenance Mindset

While air travel is faster, more efficient, and safer than ever before, we still need to contend with gravity – the Earth's unrelenting pull on all physical objects.

Therefore, to keep air travel safe, those in air transportation vigilantly maintain aircraft. While they might never change the engine in their car, you can be sure they replace aircraft engines on a routine basis ... whether it needs it or not. After all, being stranded on US-41 is no big deal but being stalled at 10,000 feet is.

So, as you cultivate the relationships within your growing network, care for them as you would maintain an airplane. Don't wait for a relationship to be broken before you tend to it.

Never chance that something might go wrong. Rather, routinely reach out to the important people in your life, whether personal or professional. See how they're doing. And in so doing, you'll show that you care. That will serve to keep your entire fleet of relationships airborne.

## -61-
## Magnets And Pushers

As author and consultant Paul Edwards says in his popular book, *Business Beyond Business*, "The difference between a pusher and a 'magnet' is that magnets create gravitational 'pull' that draws people towards them."

Edwards goes on to write that "pushers see people more like transactions to be carried out." The pusher believes that someone has money, and they seek to get it. While the exchange is generally fair – money for a product or service – the pusher mindset is one of "what can this person do for me right now?"

Edwards indicates that magnets are different. They see people as untapped reservoirs of knowledge, ideas, passion, dreams and connections, in exchange for similar resources and energy.

With that, today, stop and look around. When you see someone new, see a wealth of long-term mutual potential. See a person with whom you can exchanges contacts, thoughts and opportunities. If you condition yourself to do this, you'll have the power to attract people to you.

# -62-
# Network Building From 1,000 Acts

In China for the better part of a 1,000 years, the government practiced a form of torture known as "death from a 1,000 Cuts." Under this form of execution, the convicted person was not killed mercifully. Rather the villain was executed by a series of daily small incisions. These collectively over time spelled doom for the condemned.

Establishing a strong network is truly the reverse of this. You successfully build a network by consistently performing literally thousands of small and seemingly insignificant acts.

You flash a big, happy smile thousands of times. You perform thousands of kind acts. You exhibit reliability with unfailing consistency thousands of times. No one smile, or single kind act, or individual demonstration of dependability has any significance in and of itself. Collectively, however, they have an immense power to build your network.

Knowing that it takes thousands of insignificant acts to build a great network, continually ask yourself, "What seemingly, meaningless network building act am I doing right now?"

## -63-
## Courageously Forge Ahead

Know this, if you don't already: As you embark upon success, not everyone will be firmly behind you.

There will be well-intentioned people holding you back because they don't truly understand what it is you are after. They'll say things like, "You better not; you might get hurt."

And there will be people pulling you back because they are so afraid that you are going to achieve something that they won't. They will attempt to assert peer pressure to deter you with criticism, such as "that's a waste of time" or "you're such a workaholic."

Sure, it can be difficult to forge ahead in the wake of these detractors, especially when some of them are family and friends. Nevertheless, put on blinders, insert earplugs and courageously forge ahead.

Success is a special thing. And it's special, in part, because you're willing to take on challenges even when it feels like you're all alone.

# -64-
# Life Is Choices

"Life is choices. We are constantly making decisions, and the decisions we make today determine who we become tomorrow." These are the words of Matthew Kelly, *New York Times* bestselling author, speaker, and a business consultant.

Kelly is right. Every moment of life is a choice. You choose to listen to this program. You've chosen to continue. You'll choose whether to take action on what you hear or not. Every moment is a choice.

But also remember that each and every choice leads to something. Good choices raise you up and lead to better opportunities. And these opportunities offer you better options to choose from.

On the other hand, bad choices lead to objectionable challenges. And these challenges present you with undesirable options to choose from.

Remember, success comes from a string of great choices. One by one they build to something wonderful. With that, endeavor to make good choices.

## -65-
## Focusing on Being Your Best

It's a natural human tendency, isn't it? You know, to look over your shoulder to see what the other person has got. Thoughts flow through your mind like …

I wonder if I'm in better shape.
Or I wonder if their house is worth more.
Or I wonder if they make more than I do.

While these ponderings seem to be natural, that doesn't mean you shouldn't work to push these thoughts aside. You know, focus on you. On what you have. On what more you're looking to achieve.

This is the reality: It does nothing for you to compare yourself to anyone else. After all, no two situations are alike. You have a unique path to this point in time and as such comparing outcomes is pointless.

Never compare yourself to anyone else. Just focus on being your best and doing your best. Not necessarily "the" best, just your best. Great things will follow from that alone.

## -66-
## Call It Old-Fashion, But ...

Although the computer has made it easier than ever to send letters or blast out e-mails at the speed of light, the handwritten note endures as a wonderful means to make a lasting impression.

Sure, some believe that it's the practice of someone who simply doesn't want to join the 21st century. But in reality, the handwritten note is emblematic of someone who wants to put forth a little bit of humanity.

Nothing brings on a smile like a handwritten note. And nothing encourages people to pause and reflect like reading a handwritten note. And nothing creates friendship like a handwritten note.

You see, a handwritten note makes a powerful and lasting impression on the recipient. They feel as if they matter enough for you to take the time to give your own personal touch related to a few words of remembrance. And, for that reason, the handwritten note will always be a valued, respected, and honored form of communication.

## -67-
## Plant Trees You'll Never See

In his book *No One Gets There Alone*, Dr. Rob Bell, author, speaker, and sports psychologist, shares a phrase: Plant Trees You Will Never See.

In sharing the phrase, he goes on to encourage us to conduct ourselves so that we aren't just doing things for the moment or some hopeful payback. Rather he encourages that we add value to the world in such a manner that we serve to create a legacy.

Yes, lifting up the life of someone you know is certainly a respectable act of generosity. However, working to lift up the life of someone you don't know and may well never see again rises to a whole new level of nobility.

Planting trees that you will never see means adding value to the world – not because there is something in it for you – but rather because it's the right thing to do.

## -68-
## Everything You Say, You Need To Hear

You're a leader, right? Whether it's a large company, or a decent-sized team of people or just a small somebody needing your guidance. Whomever, however, you play the role of a mentor.

No doubt, in this position you share ideas, thoughts and wisdom. Great! That's an important aspect to the role.

Here's the reality, however: Everything you say, you need to hear. Think about that.

When you encourage someone with words like "keep working hard," that message also applies to you.

When you cheer on another with a pep talk like, "hang in there; things will get better," that is some medicine you also need to take from time to time.

When you guide another with wisdom such as, "be sure to have a clear vision and set definitive goals to get there," that sage advice works the same for you.

As a leader, you endeavor to inspire others with words. Remember to listen to those words too.

## -69-
## Habits Make You

Frederick Matthias Alexander once said, "People do not necessarily decide their futures, they decide their habits and their habits decide their futures."

An Australian actor who developed an educational process that helped people recognize and overcome habitual limitations – FM Alexander said this over 100 years ago. And this notion is now widely accepted. Your habits make you.

Knowing this, take an honest inventory of your routine actions and behaviors.

Are you quick to anger? Do you procrastinate at times? Do you find that you shrink from certain challenges or situations? Do you fail to follow through?

If you're having an issue with any one of these (or any one of two dozen more), know that you can absolutely change the trajectory of your life by simply working to change a habit. Find a habit you can easily correct and do so. Then move on to the next. In time, your new habits will serve to make you into something great.

# -70-
## No Vision, No Achievement

Author, speaker and personal development influencer, Lewis Howes, remarked in his book *The School of Greatness*, "If you don't give yourself a moment to visualize the clear results you want to create, then you are less likely to achieve what you desire."

Stop. Take a moment to think. Where do you want to be five years from now? Five months? Five weeks?

> What would you like to achieve?
> What do you stand for?
> Who do you have surrounding you?
> What legacy are you creating?

Stop and take a moment to think. Today. And tomorrow. And the day after that. And every day going forward. Sure, the ultimate vision might shift depending upon your progress and changing dreams, but it's important to consistently take a moment to envision what your hopes and dreams look like.

Without consistently fixing your mind on what your ultimate achievement destination will be, you impair your ability to get there.

# -71-
# Sears To Wal-Mart and Beyond

In 1962, the retail giant Sears, Roebuck and Company was poised to celebrate its 100<sup>th</sup> anniversary. Its annual sales were somewhere north of $10 billion dollars, and it was starting to expand throughout North America and beyond. That same year, Sam Walton opened the first Wal-Mart Discount Store in tiny Rogers, Arkansas.

Fast forward to today. One of these is a household name, with millions of employees, and annual sales of over a half a trillion dollars. The other is now virtually unknown by much of the population and a punchline for those who remember it.

This is more than an interesting contrast. There are a couple lessons to be had. First, don't ever let anyone tell you that you can't out-work, out-think, and out-execute a competitor that is much bigger than you.

Second, no matter how your professional life grows, don't ever get into the mindset that you don't have to innovate and improve.

# -72-
# Managing Challenges

In the book *The Power of Full Engagement: Managing Energy, Not Time, Is The Key To High Performance and Personal Renewal*, authors Jim Loeher and Tony Schwartz offer simple ideas to prevent challenges from taking you down.

Idea 1: Write down the perceived threats and then recast them as opportunities. Through this exercise you will likely realize that, despite the perceived challenges, good can come from the situation.

Idea 2: Regarding the perceived threats, think through the likely worst-case scenario. With this, you may realize that the perceived threat might be more to your ego than a real risk of loss.

Idea 3: Make a list of the things in your life that are going well. Doing this, you'll take your mind off the challenges and create a renewed appreciation for all you really do have.

While none of these exercises serves to make the challenges go away, each serves to put the challenge in perspective.

## -73-
## Results Matter

In a 2019 issue of *Success Magazine*, Tony Jeary, also known as The Results Guy, shared his thoughts on how you can make the most out of any day. He indicates that it starts by being intentional relative to a few key things.

One, each day make a good to-do list that you'll follow through on.

Two, become organized so that you know where things are on your desk, on your computer and throughout your office.

Three, schedule your time on your calendar. If something potentially intervenes, say NO to it, unless it's a grave emergency or an incredible opportunity.

Finally, constantly audit yourself. Jeary encourages that at the end of each day you make an honest assessment. Ask yourself, "How did I do? Was I productive or simply consumed with busy work?"

He reminds us that activities that don't lead to results are considered low leverage. These should be minimized, if not eliminated. Remember, activities don't count. Only results matter.

# -74-
# A Perfect Mistake

On June 10th, 2010, Detroit Tigers' pitcher Armando Galarraga was only two outs away from pitching the perfect game. This is one of the rarest of achievements in major league baseball – facing 27 batters and retiring 27 batters in the same game.

Unfortunately for Galarraga, the first-base umpire, Jim Joyce, made a mistake. He called a runner safe at first base when the replay clearly showed he was out. The perfect game was lost.

After the game, players and fans were outraged at Joyce. They demanded the umpire's termination or suspension. Tensions were high.

Realizing he'd made an errant call Joyce made an uncharacteristic move. He went out of his way to find and apologize to Galarraga. In turn, the young pitcher made a public declaration of forgiveness. These gestures served to defuse the situation.

The lesson is simple. In time you'll be wronged and in time you do wrong. Always be open to contrition. And always be open to forgiveness.

# -75-
# Relationship Bank Account

Every relationship is like a bank account. Everything you do (or don't do, for that matter) either contributes to the relationship or draws from it.

Positive interaction (such as providing a favor or giving a compliment) tends to add to the account. Negative interaction (such as a confrontation or missing an appointment) tends to create withdrawals.

If your relationship with a particular person is strong, the account is flush. This relationship has been marked by mostly positive interactions.

On the other hand, if your relationship is merely neutral, the account has a zero balance. The interactions in this relationship are relatively equally mixed between positive and negative, or there may be no interactions at all.

If, however, your relationship is strained or worse, the account is overdrawn to some extent. The relationship has been largely marked by negative interaction.

Whether a relationship account is flush, overdrawn or somewhere in between, you need to remember that relationships are bank accounts that you need to manage.

## -76-
## Stay In Touch

Author and speaker, Matt Ward's number one rule for garnering referrals from your contacts is simple: Stay in touch.

In his popular book, *MORE … Word of Mouth Referrals, Lifelong Customers and Raving Fans*, he shares: "Regardless of how much you think you might be bothering someone, if you fail to stay in touch, you will fail to get referrals. On the contrary, though, if you find unique ways to reach out to contacts, you will get more referrals."

Ward explains that constantly reaching out or doing things to get on people's radar makes you top of mind and positions you to receive more referrals.

This then begs the question: Who in your world might be a better source of referrals and introductions for you? Think about it. Come up with a list of perhaps 10 to 12 names. Then follow Ward's advice and develop a plan to uniquely and consistently stay in touch.

## -77-
## Don't Talk Yourself Out of Networking

On the one hand, networking is a perfectly natural thing. It's merely interacting with others to create mutual benefits. It's something that humans have been doing since we first walked the grassy plains of this planet.

On the other hand, networking in the modern world is vastly different than what our ancestors did. Eons ago, early humans lived within small tribes or clans of 150 people or so and seldom if ever encountered someone from outside their world.

So, while you're hardwired to interact, it can also be naturally daunting to thrust yourself amongst total strangers. That said, you can't live in the past. You have to work through any apprehension.

Yes, often getting out and networking can seem like a daunting task. Do it anyway. Amongst those strangers before you are friends, valuable referral partners, clients, sources of information and much, much more.

Put your fear aside and capitalize on the opportunity.

## -78-
## Finish Like You Start

When you encounter someone new, how does that interaction unfold?

You make solid eye contact. It's not a stare, but a definite connecting look where you acknowledge them, right?

From there, you smile. Not a cheesy, forced grin. But rather a genuine smile, one that seems to really comes from the heart.

Then, with the foundation of eye contact and a warm smile, you extend your hand to meet theirs. This handshake is neither a bone crushing exchange nor a loose grasp that makes you wonder if it happened at all. Rather, this handshake is a firm connection of your hand web to theirs.

From here, other polite pleasantries ensue. Introductions. A little small talk. Perhaps it then rolls into business. And if all goes well you settle on a game plan for follow-up interaction.

Then this new connection finishes exactly like it starts: With a warm smile, a firm handshake and solid eye contact.

# -79-
# The Universal Currency

"What kind of currency is more valued than a hundred-dollar bill, more compact than a quarter and accepted in every country?"

Jason Treu poses this question in his best-selling book, *Social Wealth: How to Build Extraordinary Relationships By Transforming the Way We Live, Love and Network*. And the answer is simple: Social Capital.

Social capital is the intrinsic value of the personal relationships within your network. These relationships serve to bolster your position in life by providing you with personal and professional opportunities, additional wonderful contacts, and ideas and insights.

As Treu continues, "The greater your social capital, the more opportunities, access and resources you will have to get what you want in life, the more relationships you will have, and the faster your relationships will progress."

In summary, the people you interact with serve to put money in your pocket. It's not necessarily direct, but the more and better people you associate with the greater your eventual wealth.

# -80-
# Subsequent Impressions

You've probably heard the saying, "You never get a second chance to make a first impression." Certainly, it's sage advice. The first impression you make with others is important. After all, you want to start any relationship, whether personal or professional, in a positive, impactful manner.

And while your first impression is important, what's vital to a productive, long-lasting relationship are the subsequent encounters. Think about it.

There have been times where someone has made a great first impression on you. They looked the part and said all the right things. But then the more you got to know them, the less you got to like or trust them.

In contrast, you've had times where the first encounter was off for whatever reason. But in a subsequent encounter, you sensed that your initial impression might have been inaccurate. And as time wore on, it got better and better.

Yes, make a good first impression. But also ensure that all subsequent encounters are as good or better.

# -81-
# Questions To Ignite Small Talk

Small talk gets the networking process going and is most effective when you get the other person talking. There is no magic to making this happen. It's simply a matter of having a small handful of questions ready to ask. A few of these questions could include...

What do you do? How long have you been doing it? How did you become interested in that?

What are some of the projects or assignments you are currently working on?

Are you from this area? If, not, what brought you here?

Outside of work, what occupies you? How did you become interested in that?

What are some business or community organizations you are involved with?

These will give you a start. From here you might want to formulate your own series of questions. Again, there is no magic. It is simply a matter of planning on how you will get and keep them talking.

## -82-
## Poised, Confident and Focused

In his book *The Next One Up Mindset: How To Prepare For The Unknown*, mental performance coach Grant Parr shared that throughout much of his high school and collegiate football playing career he had the habit of writing the letters "P, C and F" on his taped wrist.

The letters stood for poised, confident, and focused. These served as a constant reminder, whether he was a starter or riding the bench, that he shouldn't lament what isn't, nor should he get consumed with the chaos around him. Rather, he should remain entirely focused on being ready to do his best when his moment arrived.

Parr shares that insight with both his athlete and corporate clients. You might not be a starter or have the best professional situation. None of that, however, stands in the way of getting yourself ready so that when your moment arrives, you can deliver your best performance. Poised, Confident and Focused!

# -83-
# Only A Warm and Fuzzy

Everyone is generous to one degree or another, at some point in time. And that includes you, right?

However, when you are looking to serve those around you through the goods and services you sell, this is not one of those generous moments. It's great business, for sure. You should always strive to serve your customers and clients well.

It's just not altruistic. You see, no matter how noble your profession or how passionate you are towards it, if you're compensated for your efforts, even in the slightest way, your gesture becomes transactional. At that point, much, if not all, of the generosity is stripped away.

True altruism is doing something beneficial for another with the all-important caveat that you have absolutely no expectation of getting something in return, except for perhaps that warm and fuzzy feeling that comes with the gesture.

## -84-
## Your Moral Compass

In his book *Winners Never Cheat: Everyday Values We Learned As Children (But May Have Forgotten)* American businessman, billionaire and philanthropist Jon M. Huntsman wrote:

"It sometimes takes great courage to follow the moral compass in the face of marketplace pressures, but no challenge alters this fact: Regardless of who is holding the compass, or how they are holding it, or what time of day it happens to be, north is always north, and south is always south. Following one's moral compass is not for the faint of heart or the cold of feet."

Yes, Huntsman, is right, the pressures of life can be incredible at times. From that, the incentive to gain an unfair advantage is ever present. Despite this, keep a watchful eye on your moral compass at every turn and commit to doing the right thing.

Sure, it takes a bit more effort and you'll endure some short-term setbacks, but in the end, you'll be much more respected and further ahead for it.

## -85-
## The Service Effect

Michael Rogers, president of Teamwork and Leadership, introduces the concept of the *service effect* in his book, *You Are The Team: 6 Simple Ways Teammates Can Go From Good to Great*.

According to Rogers, the *service effect* is the positive impact that occurs when people begin to serve others. In summary, as you serve, you start to love and care more about those you serve. And then as your feelings of love and caring increase, your desire to serve is further amplified.

Serve more; love more. Love more; serve more. As Rogers points out, the initial act of service is a foundation that builds and builds.

You need no invitation or signal from another to set the service effect in motion in your life. You just need to do something of service. That will infuse your heart with a little bit of love. From there you'll be inspired to do a little more. And then the effect will only build from there.

## -86-
## Who, What, Why and How

The end game of networking is to build your life with help from others. Now to get this help, you need to effectively communicate to those you know.

WHO you are? And your business name. Your products or services.

WHAT you do? And what are the situations when your products or services are utilized.

WHY should they do business with you? Or WHY should they recommend you as opposed to recommending other options (or nothing at all)?

And HOW can they help you? Who are people you want to be referred to? Who do you want to meet? What information do you need?

The primary limitation to communicating all this (especially amongst people you are meeting for the first time) is simply ATTENTION SPAN. You see, people you talk to are not going to allow you to yammer on endlessly.

So, you need to work to compact all of this into a message that is somewhere around 30 seconds long.

# -87-
# Powering Up

Others want to associate with you most when you project confidence and optimism. Knowing that, you'll want to adopt a mindset that inspires you to walk taller and have a bounce in your step.

Here's the problem. It is easy to say, "Think confident, optimistic, and powerful thoughts and that will come through as who you are." However, when you find yourself in that real-life situation surrounded by business icons, thinking this way isn't always easy.

Fortunately, researchers have found that you can easily get yourself in this confident frame of mind. Here's the trick: If you want to project a feeling of power and control, assume a high-power pose, like standing tall with your hands on your hips, not unlike Superman.

A minute or so of this and powerful psychological forces take hold. A "take charge" attitude wells up inside you. And from this, you will naturally start to feel in control ... confident ... optimistic. So, hands on hips and power up.

# -88-
# Generosity On Your Personal Ledger

Author, speaker, and persuasion expert Brian Ahearn writes in his book *Influence PEOPLE,* "I'm not advocating give to get. People are put off by those who only help in order to get something in return. I advocate giving because it's the right thing to do, the best way to live life."

Ahearn's heartfelt insight is powerful. First, there are endless ways that you can help others. Some big. Some small. Some life changing. Some simply passing gestures.

Whatever the case, when you genuinely help another person, you set in motion powerful psychological forces. While you might not expect it, the other person will genuinely want to help you when you need it. But equally important is that because you've genuinely helped first, when you really do need help you can feel good about asking for it in return.

It's comforting to know that you have both those sentiments sitting on your personal ledger, as one day they may come in handy.

## -89-
## Pounding Nails In and Out

Michael Josephson on his website *Character Counts* shared a parable about an angry nine-year-old boy who was unable to control his cruel outbursts. To help him learn self-control, his grandfather made him pound a two-inch-long nail into a four-by-four board every time he said something mean.

This was a major task for the small boy. He started to become more cautious with his words and even started to apologize for his outbursts.

Then the grandfather instructed him to pull all nails out. This was even harder than pounding them in. With that, the grandfather told the boy, "I appreciate and accept your apology, but I want you to know an apology is like pulling out these nails. Look at the board. The holes are still there. The board will never be the same."

You need to be careful with what you say. While you can certainly apologize for angry outbursts, your harsh words can have a lasting impact.

## -90-
## Never Stop Giving

The million-dollar question in networking is "How Do I Go About Getting Others To Know, Like & Trust Me?" An easy answer is focus on giving to others, as nothing will endear you to individuals in your network like making a genuine effort to help them.

Give referrals ... Give additional contacts ... Give opportunities ... Give information ... Give encouragement ... Give support ... Give, Give, Give.

When you give to others, they cannot help but come to know, like and trust you. In addition, you will develop the reputation of being a generous person. This will inspire others to want to help others too, and you'll be swept up in their wonderful spirit of generosity.

So, with every person you encounter, ask yourself, "In what way could I help them?" When the answers come to you, take action. That will build know, like, and trust like nothing else. And this answer to the million-dollar question will in time yield you a similar return.

# -91-
# Use The 15-Minute Rule

Deadlines tend to drive results. Think about it. Few people fail to get their taxes in on time. Why? There's a hard deadline with the IRS on the other end of it.

But what about the projects that don't have such a deadline. Like outlining that book you've been intending to write. There is no deadline, so how do you drive that to completion?

In her book, *Happier at Home: Kiss More, Jump More, Abandon a Project, Read Samuel Johnson, and My Other Experiments in Everyday Life*, author Gretchen Rubin encourages using the 15-Minute Rule.

She suggests earmarking 15 minutes to work on that deadline-less project. Then when the time comes, pour yourself into it. At the end of 15 minutes, stop. Do no more. But find another 15 minutes the next day.

Do this every day for a stretch, say a week. Mark your progress. According to Rubin, you'll be amazed at what you can accomplish.

# -92-
# Nothing Defines You

No doubt, you've had setbacks. We all do. It's part of life. And when they happen, well-meaning people might encourage you with a reminder that this shortcoming doesn't define you.

They're right. That horrible moment. Those embarrassing circumstances. The situation where you were completely overlooked. None of those things defines you or labels you as anything.

What does define you, however, is how you react to what happens.

Your reaction to that horrible moment can define you as someone who is strong and resilient.

How you respond in those embarrassing circumstances can define you as someone who can laugh at them self and take life in stride.

And how you react when being completely overlooked can define you as someone who forges ahead with wonderful passion and a great attitude despite the circumstances.

Nothing that happens to you defines you. Nothing. What defines you is simply you. It's you. You and how you react to the circumstances that life presents you with.

# -93-
# Huggers, Shakers, and Patters

There is something reassuring about hearing someone's voice, as opposed to reading a text or an e-mail. It's even better when you're in the same room, face to face. After all, body language communicates so much more than words and it's eye contact that serves to create the foundation for trust.

But beyond hearing and seeing, there's something special about human touch. Yes, a compassionate voice is comforting, and body language will indicate that it's real. But done appropriately, a firm handshake, a sincere pat on the shoulder or a warm hug shared with another builds a stronger sense of rapport.

Remember a successful life is neatly woven together with a litany of wonderful relationships where there is a mutual sense of knowing, liking and trusting. And, if you're looking to amplify your relationships, consider becoming a hugger, a shaker, or a patter.

## -94-
## Newton's Law and Networking

In her book *Rainmaker Roadmap: A Step-by-Step Guide to Building a Prosperous Business*, author, speaker, and consultant Kimberly Rice addresses a common occurrence when building and growing a healthy network. That is, the uncertainty surrounding when and why you reach out to your network and what to say when you do.

In response, Rice draws on Newton's law of motion: "For every action, there is an equal and opposite reaction." In networking terms, the more goodwill you extend, the more it will come back to you.

She shares that your "reaching out" messages should have a helpful spirit, with the true intention of checking in. Checking in on your contact's business. Or seeing how they are making out with a recent transition or new position. Or following up on something personal in their life.

So, add a little physics to your networking skills with Newton's law of motion. Sincerely reach out to someone. And then expect an equal and opposite reaction.

## -95-
## The Wisdom of Crowds

In 1907, Francis Galton performed a social experiment. He randomly asked attendees at a county fair to guess the weight of a particular ox. No one guessed correctly. The average of all the guesses, however, was surprisingly close to the exact weight of the ox. In fact, the average was closer to the true weight than any individual guess.

From this, the social sciences coined the phrase, "The Wisdom of Crowds." Essentially, no one person is smarter than a collection of people. And they've demonstrated this in study after study.

The lesson for you is this: No doubt, you're intelligent and well-studied. But remember, as smart as you might be, you're just one person.

In your network, however, is a collection of people. And maybe no one amongst that group is smarter than you. But amongst that crowd is great wisdom. So, don't be afraid to reach out to it and poll it for answers to challenges that plague you.

## -96-
## A Daily Dose of Social Media

To successfully engage yourself in social media (such as LinkedIn, Facebook, or Twitter), you only need to devote about 100 hours per year to it. When you put it that way, the task seems insurmountable.

Here is the reality: That translates to only about 20 minutes a day or a couple hours scattered over the course of a week. Now, that doesn't seem so bad, does it? Think about it.

In the morning, while enjoying a cup of coffee, you might tinker with your profile.

Another day take a mid-morning break and interact within one of the groups you've joined.

Then, at some point during the week, while waiting for dinner to warm up (or arrive), jump into a discussion.

Finally, when there is a break in the action from the big game you are watching, share an update.

Remember, social media is like a networking vitamin. Be sure to get your daily dose of it.

# -97-
# Networking Versus Schmoozing

As author Diane Darling shares in her bestselling book *The Networking Survival Guide: Practical Advice to Help You Gain Confidence, Approach People, and Get the Success You Want*, networking is sometimes dismissed as "schmoozing, and thus has the connotation of creating a very superficial connection that benefits only the schmoozer."

Darling goes on to explain that schmoozing is a situation where the schmoozer is out solely for themselves. They are looking to take, and nothing else. And that's not networking.

Networking is an ongoing relationship that has its foundation firmly established in mutual benefit. This is not to say that networking is a tit-for-tat exchange or transaction. It does mean, however, that each side of a networking relationship has their eyes and ears continually open for things that could benefit the other.

And while in the networking relationship there might not be a continual flow of benefit, the parties come through for one another on a consistent basis.

Darling's lesson is simple: Never schmooze; Always Network!

# -98-
# It's All Personal

If you've been out in the working world long enough, you've likely heard the phrase, "It's not personal; it's just business." This phrase implies that when unpleasant things happen, you should push the emotion aside and move forward with an indifferent, "Oh well."

Never use this phrase. Never rely on it to soften the tough realities that life sometimes requires. Why? Simple.

As humans, we each only have one brain. And while it's an amazing thing, allowing us to talk and listen, the brain cannot differentiate between business and personal.

So, in business, when you must make a difficult decision that impacts others or deliver unpleasant news to someone, know this: The person affected feels it in a very personal way. That's the only way their brain is capable of processing the impact.

None of this suggests avoiding these unpleasantries. To be successful, you can't. What it does encourage, however, is that you handle them with empathy.

## -99-
## A Lifetime of Happiness

There is a Chinese Proverb that goes: If you want happiness for an hour, take a nap. If you want happiness for a day, go fishing. If you want happiness for a month, get married. If you want happiness for a year, inherit a fortune. If you want happiness for a lifetime, help others.

There are so many ways for you to help others. Give them referrals. Introduce them to others. Share information with them. Listen to their challenges. Encourage them when they're down. Celebrate their successes.

And there are so many ways helping others will bring you happiness. You'll have people to give you referrals. As you introduce them, they'll want to introduce you. They have insightful information that will benefit you too. They have ears that'll be open to hear your troubles. When you're down, they'll spur you on. And when you achieve, they'll cheer loudest of all.

Bring happiness into your life. Help someone today!

## -100-
## Referrals Beget Referrals

In his book *Beyond Referrals: How To Use the Perpetual Revenue System to Convert Referrals into High-Value Clients*, best-selling author Bill Cates shares his thoughts on the litany of benefits that referrals offer. One is that referrals beget referrals. Cates shares:

"A client obtained through a referral is more likely to give referrals. And since many clients will give you multiple referrals over time, your business growth is exponential."

Yes, Cates is correct, one referral leads to more and more referrals. For this reason, if you're in business you should invest time into activities that build referral opportunities.

Make time to attend events where you can be known and get to know others.

Volunteer your time in the community (and allot time for your team to do the same).

Take the time to do something extraordinary for significant contacts and clients on their special days.

Invest this time in referral opportunities, as the rate of return is unmatched.

# -101-
# It's Okay to Talk to Strangers

Next time you're at a networking event … or really any place where people congregate … look around. Do you see that person you don't know?

That person is someone with a history to them. They have experiences. They have insights. They have a network of people you don't even know exist. So, don't see them as a stranger. Rather, see them as a potential colleague, a center of influence, or a friend. That person represents real opportunity for you … and you hold the same opportunities for them.

So, take the initiative. Go up to them and introduce yourself. In this sense, it's okay to talk to strangers because in an instant they will no longer be one.

As Brian Miller shares in his book Three New People, "You have no idea what kind of opportunities await you just on the other side of the next connection."

**There you have it—101 essays. But we wanted to offer a bonus essay. Before we do, if you're interested in exploring other books, content, and programs by Frank Agin, visit frankagin.com or simply search "Frank Agin" on whatever platform you use to get great content.**

# -102-
# Keep Shooting

Take a minute and think about that person you really aspire to. WOW! To be like them would be awesome, right? Who wouldn't want to be that big shot?

Here's the thing. Whoever they are. Whatever stratosphere they currently occupy, they were once pretty much in the same position you are today. Maybe worse. What happened? Simple. It goes like this, "All a big shot is, is a little shot who just kept shooting."

So, they were just like you. But they kept going. You can claim, "No, they caught a break." The reality is that they made that break ... just by continuing to shoot. When they hit upon some success, they kept shooting. When they meet with failure – whether big or small – they kept shooting. And on those long, ho-hum days they kept shooting.

So, if you want to be that big shot, you just need to keep shooting.

## About The Author

Frank Agin is president of AmSpirit Business Connections, which empowers entrepreneurs, sales representatives, and professionals to become successful and gain more referrals through networking.

He also shares information and insights on professional relationships, business networking and best practices for generating referrals on his Networking Rx podcast and through various professional programs.

Finally, Frank is the author of several books, including *Foundational Networking: Building Know, Like & Trust to Create a Life of Extraordinary Success*. See all his books and programs at frankagin.com. You can reach him at frankagin@amspirit.com.